CW00486045

Acknowledgements

The publication of this book was made possible by funding from the NERC grant Greenhouse gAs Uk and Global Emissions (GAUGE). NERC Reference: NE/K002279/1. Thank you to Professor Paul Palmer for believing in this project and for being such a generous supporter, to Matt Girling for the amazing cover art, and to Anna Frew, who did an incredible job in editing and typesetting this book. Thank you also to Sarah Haywood from the Environmental Justice Foundation for all of her help and input. Finally, thank you to all of the authors and indeed to everyone who entered the competition which preceded this book, without whom none of this would have been possible.

Editorial

Climate change is real. It is happening now. It effects all of us. And the only way that we can mitigate its effects in a meaningful fashion is to take collective action. Part of the challenge that we face in mobilising this collective action is in convincing people from currently less affected areas that climate change is right now, this very second, responsible for the destruction of thousands of ecosystems, insects, animals, plants, birds, and humans. What is needed is something that can transcend cultural barriers, and which can contextualise and localise a global problem. What is needed is poetry.

In the summer of 2017, we initiated a global poetry competition. A challenge to find 20 poems that spoke about climate change in different voices, and which would help to make real this global, interdisciplinary problem. The only stipulations that we set were that the poems had to be about climate change (however the author might perceive this) and that they had to be 40 lines or less. We received 174 entries from 23 countries in five different languages, and after a rigorous selection process 20 poems were chosen, the result of which is this book: *A Change of Climate*. Some of the poems in this collection are sad, some of them are angry, some of them are even funny. But all of them are real. Real poems from real people about the very real topic of climate change.

As Helen Mort notes in her foreword to this book: talking about climate change is difficult. Even experts find it challenging to establish a common language that communicates their research, statistics, and emotions effectively. Poetry presents an opportunity for people to express themselves in a different way, to find a fitting language that enables them to talk about climate change in a manner that is personable to them, one which can help them to make sense of this global problem in a very local context.

All of the profits from this book will go to the Environmental Justice Foundation (EJF), an organisation that works hard to protect both our people and our planet, by campaigning for human rights and the rights of the environment. EJF investigate and expose environmental and human rights abuses through film and photography and by purchasing this book, you are helping to support their Climate Campaign, which is centred on fighting for the rights of climate refugees. We hope that you enjoy reading the poems that are collected within this book, and that through reading them you are able to find your own voice in relation to climate change. A voice that you can then use to take the collective action that is needed to save our people and our planet.

Dr Sam Illingworth & Mr Dan Simpson
www.illingworthandsimpson.com

Visions of Unwanted Futures

Climate change is the focus of my research, and as the co-chair for the Working Group 1 on the Intergovernmental Panel on Climate Change (IPCC) I am coordinating a tremendous scientific endeavour. One in which hundreds of volunteer scientists from diverse backgrounds are collectively assessing the state of knowledge in climate and climate change sciences, and distilling their key findings for policy-makers.

Climate change is my scientific homeland, and I have long explored various options to share my fascination for climate sciences and their implications with children, with onlookers, and with those who are impervious to numbers, maps and graphs.

How can we share the history of climate science, the discoveries and challenges, the scientific facts, and the open questions? How can we share the outcomes of climate science so that they can percolate into the general culture? How can we build bridges across knowledge approaches and systems, across visions of the world? How can we share our sense of urgency and catalyse transformations?

I usually refer to climate change as an impressionist painting: you need to look at it from a distance to be able to distinguish the overall picture from the juxtaposition of individual colour splashes. Unfortunately, our daily life facilitates a zoom on these individual colour splashes: we undergo local and short-term weather and cannot directly perceive global and long-term changes; the flow of information brings patchy news which do not facilitate understanding; alarmist approaches attract attention, but coping with anxiety fuels denial; and merchants of doubt deploy their skills to blur the bigger picture.

Scientists themselves are challenged in their abilities to communicate their findings. In our work life, scientific rigor and accuracy are crucial. But scientific jargon and the language of uncertainty are not always our most useful allies when we want to share our knowledge with a wider audience. When presenting key findings of climate science assessments, I have often joked and said that scientists are not poets.

I was wrong.

Sam Illingworth, who is an atmospheric scientist, is exploring poetry as a vector to communicate scientific research in an engaging manner. I am very honoured that he asked me to write this foreword.

I have repeatedly been impressed by the complementarity of art and sciences. Science is about reason, about understanding our world, about objectively building and structuring knowledge in a verifiable manner. Art is about senses, emotions, representations and symbols, dialogue and beauty. I see beauty in science, when methodologies are elegant; and some see an art in methods of climate science and in scientific assessments...

The 20 winning poems assembled in this book provide stunning visions of *A Change of Climate*.

Your journey will start by thoughts of bees and their 'giant furred white bear version', polar bears, together with hopes for heritage and survival for 'something old and more than human.'

It is followed by the awkward silence of an impossible conversation, which I understand to reflect the challenges to make climate change issues barge into the daily life. Why aren't we prepared to manage risks? People from the Leeward Islands were recently hit by a category 5 hurricane ironically named Irma, as a 'clairvoyant.' The tribute to these people dives into the disaster shock, and stresses our misperception of invulnerability when watching ravages 'from a balcony believed to be strong.'

Solutions exist, and hope is expressed in 'SLAG', stressing that you can like different things, including what can be perceived as a nuisance. It describes the nostalgia for a past marked by a dark love of coal and the silence of canaries, time passing by, and new love for a different world, with bird songs and wind turbines 'slicing clean paths to a future'.

A bitter fact is that we are sabotaging oceans of all types. 'We are no longer interested in the sea' suggests that we should be more proactive, and ironically incites us to get rid of it, to fill completely the sea with our waste, to solidify it. Similarly, our plastic waste is agglomerating into oceans, entering into the food chain. 'Swimming lesson' stresses that much of this waste results from toys and hygiene and beauty products, concluding that we absurdly 'want to die clean'. Over North America, rare 'Karner Blue' butterflies named by Vladimir Nabokov once created ephemeral 'landlocked seas', which have since 'dried up'.

Are we acting as lice on Gaia's head, 'millennium after millennium, drilling in (her) cranium'? She does not see any option than to ask her hairdresser, Chaos, to shave her head…

The survival of our civilization is intrinsically linked to the preservation of other forms of life on Earth. The requiem for our civilization will be played in an annual extinction concert on a piano, the keys of which will have been assembled from the bones of extinct species by visionary students. Let us image the future, if we cannot stabilize climate change. How will today's children judge our inaction? '21__' explores mermaids of the future, swimming into submerged remains of Manhattan buildings, while murmuring 'We know this for a hundred years, yet nobody did anything'.

The drama of irreversible damage is illustrated in 'The Dead Zone arranged by us', where modern Capulets and Montagues destroy fragile trees, leaving a silent and grey landscape of devastation. Exposing the illusions of a technological development leaving only rubble, 'Wandering the Anthropocene' targets greed as the root cause of multiplied damage, and calls for a radical transformation building on 'organic motivation'. We are travelling, capturing snapshots of landscapes, but 'The Earth's Plea' is lucid, we are not aware of the deep destruction at play, we are not aware of the close interplay between thriving ecosystems and thriving human beings. 'Only you hold the power to save us.' This tragic disconnection between the damage at play and the inertia of our society is sharply expressed in 'Hurtling' written after hurricane Harvey, when the US Administrator of the Environmental Protection Agency said in an interview that "the time to talk about climate change is not now".

I want to mention here the first scientific study published by Isaac Held (MIT) last month in the Proceedings of the National Academy of Sciences of the USA[1] assessing how torrential hurricane rains similar to those of Harvey would evolve in Texas in a warmer world. If greenhouse gas emissions continue to increase, the likelihood of such rains would increase from once in 100 years now to once in 5.5 years by the end of this century.

How can we redesign and reboot our system? Inspired by David Attenborough, 'Planet Earth II' offers a list of inclusive options for a 2.0 version of our life on our planet, most of which are unfortunately 'currently out of stock.'

The disbelief between science and society is illustrated by 'Needlework', a tale possibly inspired by the ozone hole, and which I imagine taking place in Latin America. If there is a hole in the sky, why could skilled ladies not simply stitch it up? Why is it perceived to be a trick from a 'gringo'? Ironically, action to mitigate ozone destruction has been a remarkable success, with recovery now expected to take place in the coming decades, following the phase-out of industrial ozone-destructive substances.

How can we destroy our home? 'Zest' provides a recipe to peel the Earth from its superficial but vital shells, one by one, ending with a dire warning. The unintended consequences of our way of life are sharply exposed by 'Crab', and its reflections from a hermit crab living in Henderson Island, in the South Pacific, one of the most remote places in the world.

---

[1] www.pnas.org/content/early/2017/11/07/1716222114.full

What is the geography of a changing climate? What is knowledge, and how to describe and share it? How can we explain to school children that 'the greatest losses start in smaller'? How can we share the deep interconnections between economy, climate change, and people? The need for introspection is brightly explored in 'Geography Lessons'.

Finally, 'Eschaton' explores an apocalyptic return of Christ in 'a murdered Earth', destroyed by climate change, 'with no-one left to save except the jellyfish', describing hell as 'a muddy, wet place'. In 2017 alone, more than 41 million people were affected by floods in South Asia.

Science is clear. Our sources of energy and food, by releasing heat-trapping gases, are causing global warming, rising seas, and already more extreme events such as heat waves and heavy rainfall, threatening habitats and living conditions for us and for many other species. There are multiple options to act now and build a development which is more inclusive and resilient to climate change, while decreasing emissions of greenhouse gases; but this needs to happen as quickly as possible to reduce further losses and damage. Visions of futures that we do not want can help accelerate this action.

I hope that you will enjoy reading these 20 poems as much as I did.

I hope that you may also want to read some of our scientific assessments, with all your indulgence for our jargon and style[1].

Valérie Masson-Delmotte

---

[1] www.ipcc.ch

On Silence

Poetry has a special relationship with silence and - dare I say it - with a sense of inarticulacy. Perhaps I'm just speaking personally: ever since I was a child, I've been drawn to the spare, condensed form of the poem and its relationship to blank space. As Glyn Maxwell puts it in his Ars Poetica *On Poetry*:

Poets work with two materials, one's black, one's white...You want to hear the whiteness eating? Write out the lyrics of a song you love ... If you strip the music off it, it dies in the whiteness, can't breathe there.

I've been fascinated by the sense I get that I can express myself in poems in a way I can't in everyday speech or even in other written forms. For me, poetry really is a 'momentary stay against confusion', to quote Robert Frost. But poetry is also, by its very nature, an allusive (and perhaps elusive) medium. We're often striving towards the unsaid, dreaming about something that language can't quite catch in its net. The best poem for me is always the one I haven't written yet, its sense of potential and infinite possibility. This is particularly true of poetry about climate change.

In summer 2016, I spent several weeks sleeping next to the calving face of the huge Knud Rasmussen glacier in East Greenland as part of a mountaineering trip. My intention was to write about the landscape I was in, but my attempts failed again and again. These glaciers are changing at a startling rate. They have lost around nine trillion tonnes of ice in the past century and that rate of loss has only increased over time. How could I reconcile that with the beauty of the calving, the sense of mystery I felt when staring down into a crevasse or moulin? How could I write about a shifting landscape in a way that was neither overly romantic nor overly bleak?

Talking about climate change is difficult. You risk over-dramatising your subject or else seeming dry, reeling off a list of statistics. This is where poetry - with its unique capacity to hold paradox - can find a fitting language. This unique anthology showcases that to brilliant effect. In 'The Climate of Our Conversations', S.B. Banks reflects: 'the brisket / is here and I still don't know / how to have a conversation.' The narrator reflects on statistics and facts, admitting:

There are certain words I can't say.
Other words I can,
but with the risk of a sigh...

Writing about climate change comes with a risk of hypocrisy too and - again - poetry can interrogate that. As a writer from the North East Derbyshire coalfields, that's something I'm always acutely aware of. These uncomfortable juxtapositions are captured in Emily Cotterill's brilliant poem 'SLAG':

I have loved coal,
like a teenage girl loves an older guitarist
with a rough black smudge of eyeliner.

Many of the poems in this varied collection deal with the contradictions and confusions of mapping climate change through literature by adopting a surreal approach: in Michael Conley's 'We are no longer interested in the sea', people gather to pelt the oceans with stones and kitchen implements. Kim Goldberg's 'The Keys of the Piano' imagines an 'annual extinction conference.' Ben Norris' 'Planet Earth II' describes a manufactured planet:

Planet Earth II was designed in California and assembled in China
Planet Earth II is repayable in easy monthly instalments
Planet Earth II allows you to love the right person first time round

There are dystopian visions, inevitably. But they are also nuanced, wry and hopeful by their very existence - in talking about climate change through poetry, we are broadening the conversation. This collection features thrilling new work from Carrie Etter and Sarah Westcott, but it also introduced me to new voices too.

When I began the project of trying to write about (or perhaps write 'out of') East Greenland, it was clear to me that one register, one voice would never be enough. The responses in this anthology are often in different languages and represent different cultural responses to climate change, reflecting the global nature of debate. My own response was a collaboration with a filmmaker and a composer, a piece called 'The Singing Glacier'. We cast these words, images and ideas into the silence and hope to hear something back. As the poet Andrew Greig puts it:

She would say to discover
the true depth of a well,
drop a stone,
start counting.

Helen Mort

The Honey and the Polar Bear

They're still talking about the ice caps melting,
how we're headed for mass extinction. No one's listening,
or finds the time to care. We're too small and single in our
homes,
our little, warm units.

In ours, you've been coaxing honey from its comb all day.
The bees are missing their golden rivers, beginning again.
In the day's slipping away, a silent coronation.
The slow bow of evening wraps the windows in its robes.

Nine glass hexagons blush in half light and sigh.
Every surface is sticky with labour and devotion.
I've walked the house on glued feet, tangled pollen in hair,
taped sugar to lips. In the falling away of light, a summoning.

In the last exhale of evening the honey shows itself to be
gilded icon, dragon's eye, ancient offering.
Outside looking in, my face is ambered insect,
bowing monk. The room is gold, gilded, pollen-rich.

In yellow pooled corners, eddies of light drift
to ochre sea. The kitchen is gold-leaf medieval scene.
The world, for a moment, is coated in honey.
I take the burnish and pray with it, lick my finger in devotion.

How many bees hauled neon pollen
for these burning pots?
How many in the world are there, were there, have there
been?
How many will there be when the next harvest draws in?

The clear light of day is slipping away.
In the fold and fall and measure of it, evening's exhale frowns
at this ancient miracle, remembering fields of wildflowers,
cleaner air. I think of polar bears and pray a modern prayer.

I pray an ancient prayer. For the health of the hive,
for this one thing to survive,
for inheritance, durability, tenacity, safety,
something old and more than human to hold to as night
descends.

They say you should talk to bees about death, change, growth,
but the one that's stuck is death. Only I can't find the words
to tell of their dead comrades, the fallen colonies,
the giant furred white bear version of them slipping on ice on
faraway seas.

Suzi Attree

The Climate of Our Conversations

There's the table and tall plastic
menus while we wait. I watch his belly
hit the table when pulling up his chair.
Mine does the same.

Their channel's on a tv overhead,
muted, with stripes of text
that won't stop marching.
The Cowboys are on as well,
trotting across a green field
near the bar.

I try to choose my words. I try
to figure out what to say
and when.

They bring out the plates — meats
and beans and slaw and white bread
with thick paper napkins.

Back home. This is what this is.
Never knowing what to say.
How to make this better.
Us better.

There are certain words I can't say.
Other words I can,
but with the risk of a sigh,
a tilted head with *"really?"*-eyes,
and a silent drive home,
windows rolled up.

I remember reading the clever quotes and stats,
but they're gone from my head. The brisket
is here and I still don't know
how to have a conversation.

S.B. Banks

Iles du Vent

pour ceux de Saint-Martin et de Saint-Barthélémy

la maison a tremblé
et nous recroquevillés sous la table
récitant quelques bribes d'église
espérions ressortir constater les décombres

le sol a tressailli
et nous serrés tous ensemble
appelant la survie
ordonnions au progrès de dominer le sinistre

la mer a tangué
et nous bien calfeutrés
se souvenant de la vie calme pleurions pour empêcher le pire

et quand le vent a frappé
avec son nom de voyante
nous incrédules et confiants avions compris qu'il était trop
tard

du ravage naît la philosophie
mais pour beaucoup encore
il se regarde de très haut
d'une terrasse que l'on croit solide

Leeward Islands

for those of Saint Martin and Saint Barthélemy

the house shook
and we
curled up under the table
reciting some murmurs of Church
hoped to go out again
assess the damage

the ground shuddered
and we
squeezed all together
calling for survival
told the progress to prevail
over the disaster

the sea pitched
and we
well caulked
remembering the quiet life
cried out to prevent
the worst

and when the wind hit
with its name of clairvoyant
we
incredulous and confident
understood it was
too late

of the ravage arises philosophy
but we
look at it from up high
from a balcony
believed
to be strong

Camille Brantes

We are no longer interested in the sea

We are no longer interested in the sea.
The sea is a tiresome old man shouting
down dementia's cushioned corridors
and we are not fooled by its bluster. In fact

we are sick of the sea. We are sick
of its desire to relive former glories,
its gatecrashery of our parties,
its pathetic attempts at coup d'etat.

We should kill it. We should go
to the beach at night and pelt the sea
with stones until our breath pricks
our lungs like a swallowed anemone.

Bring everything you have: kettles,
refrigerators, old washing machines.
Pitch them in. Force everything we have ever built
down its open gullet and lose yourselves

in the ecstasy of it. We will drown the sea
in solidity and we will walk upon it
in our thousands. The earth and the sky
will be forced to sit up and take notice.

Michael Conley

SLAG

I have loved coal,
like a teenage girl loves an older guitarist
with a rough black smudge of eyeliner.
I have built my life on it,
screamed down decades for it,
COAL NOT DOLE –
bared my whole soul for it
but old women gossip about the pit,
I know the world has had enough of it.

Coal – with its head full of history,
strong arms, filthy engines, heavy,
the small town sex of it.
Broken bodies, white knuckle wives,
the silence of canaries – has risen
from slag heaps and pit heads
to thick air spluttering into anyone born
late with withered old miners' lungs.

I have loved coal but recently,
when I sit in the fresh place built
on the scar of my grandfather's pit
I have loved birdsong, greenspace,
the safety and hope of it –
wind turbines, rising white beacons,
sharp armed, slicing clean paths
to a future.

Emily Cotterill

Swimming lesson

We're floundering, learning properties of water:
the way plastic swims into the food chain,
bulky in albatross bellies, broken in guts
of small birds: battered by waves,
seasalt, by the sun's bleaching.

Bottle tops, Barbie shoes, lighters, toy soldiers:
the gyre gulps them all, swills and gargles them
smaller and smaller. Suspended solutions
of Lego, piled up in the organs of fish.
Once the colour has gone no-one sees.

We're counting the grains. Five trillion pieces
of plastic bags, jerry cans, spring water bottles
float in the oceans. We're filling our faces
with containers of bleach, washing up liquid,
hair products, makeup remover. We want to die clean.

Julian Dobson

(this poem originally appeared in issue 62 of *The Interpreter's House*)

Karner Blue

"...a place called Karner, where in some pine barrens,
on lupines, a little blue butterfly I have described and
named ought to be out."

Vladimir Nabokov

Because it used to be more populous in Illinois.
Because its wingspan is an inch.
Because it requires blue lupine.
Because to become blue, it has to ingest the leaves of a blue
plant.
Because its scientific name, *Lycaeides melissa samuelis*, is
mellifluous.
Because the female is not only blue but blue and orange and
silver and black.
Because its beauty galvanizes collectors.
Because Nabokov named it.
Because its collection is criminal.
Because it lives in black oak savannahs and pine barrens.
Because it once produced landlocked seas.
Because it has declined ninety per cent in fifteen years.
Because it is.

Carrie Etter

Gaia goes to the Hairdresser

Chaos capes her shoulders, *You're sure?*
I need a change, sighs Gaia, from the chair.
Catching her eye in the mirror,
Chaos knows there will be more.
Millennium after millennium,
drilling in my cranium.
At first I thought it was a teething
problem, then a teenage thing
but now I'm sick of it, sick of it –
my pores are clogged with all their shit
and, honestly, look at me –
half of it has fallen out already.

Chaos starts combing;
it's true her mane is looking thin.
But don't you think it's a bit extreme?
She shrugs, *I've tried everything.*
Pestilence? Chaos raises the clippers.
They always find a cure.
Famine? Chaos buzzes them on.
They always found an aid program.
War? Gaia shakes her head,
There's nothing for it but death.
And Chaos scythes it clean, comforting,
It'll soon grow back again.

Nathan Evans

The Keys of the Piano

The keys of the piano at the annual
extinction concert were built from bones
of vanished species—each pallid slab
a different absence in the ravelling
weft. And the people wept

as the unholy keen rose
from the cliffside amphitheatre slicing
the summer sky above the sea, clashing
chords formulated by features of
mineral density rather than
scalar math, battling the crash
of wave, the wail of gull, a thunder of
harmonics too ecstatic or demonic
to withstand. It began with a rat

back in 2016. The mosaic-
tailed rat endemic to Bramble Cay
in the Great Barrier Reef: declared the first
mammalian casualty of climate change.
And the people blinked

but recovered. Just a rat
on a small coral island barely above
sea level. Who can understand the genius
of a mind that sees music and immortality
in a cadaver? As a grad student, she flew

to Papua New Guinea and hired a boat
to collect a satchel of remains that became
the first key in the first piano in the first
annual extinction concert all those years
ago. Tonight beside the sea

spray of salt upon her aging cheek
co-mingling with greying hair, ancient
reverberations, tonal beats on an evolutionary
scale, pale skeletons defying time, space
the slow descent of civilization.

Kim Goldberg

21_ _

The waters swelling
Head above weather,
We backstroke glacial,
The long ambling reach,
All time ours.

Ruined buildings, silent witness.
Someone whispers: *Manhattan.*
We enter the fifty-first floor through a window,
Wriggle out dark like fishes

A scientist among us murmurs,
Digging up history:
We knew this for a hundred years
Yet nobody did anything.

We keep swirling, mermaids of the
Future. Earth is a forlorn shore.
Soon we touch the sky
And wade our dreams with those distant stars

Amlanjyoti Goswami

Needlework

There are holes in the sky!
The news arrives with an American tourist.
¡Imposible! says Don Pedro. Our village has a sky like a well-
made sheet! Pero,
says Don Julio, remember the rainstorm,
which washed the road away?
At the village meeting they agree:
the ladies good at darning will go to see.

The men build a tall ladder, two trees high,
shaking a twisted passage to the sky.
Gathering round, children cry.
The priest folds messages for heaven,
women clutch needles tight.
They pray as they climb, the ladies, nervous steps,
half-forgotten hymns, the sun bright.
Who knows, maybe there are others, at the top,
already stitching.

The earth grows distant, but the sky is still far.
Doña Chilo yells: I cannot see a hole!
There is no hole!
¡Este gringo nos ha engañado![1]
So the chorus goes.
¡Este gringo nos ha engañado!

---

[1] That American tricked us!

On the ground, the men work up a heat wave,
flourish flags like Northern winds, make speeches like
storms.
The ladies move to their dark homes,
sit by the window with piles of shirts,
poking at cotton scuffs.
Needles furious.

Catriona Knapman

ЗДЕСЬ МЕРТВУЮ ЗОНУ УСТРОИЛИ ЛЮДИ

1.
Без блеска, в ровном сером свете
под небом пасмурным стоят
стволы дерев – по всей планете
за рядом ряд, за рядом ряд,
как бы прощупывая чутко
живыми почками антенн
наш небосвод – такой же хрупкий, -
и опасаясь перемен.
Здесь Капулетти и Монтеки,
для них вражда – привычный труд:
придут с пилою дровосеки,
ряды зеленые падут.
И лишь тогда мы ужаснемся,
увы, отнюдь не от стыда,
на их могилах задохнемся,
уйдем за ними навсегда.

2.
Как за окнами шумела перестройка
и газетный разворачивался гам,
и летела в неизвестность птица-тройка
к показавшимся во мраке берегам.
Только снова что-то из виду пропала,
снова дальний горизонт заволокло,
окружающей среды почти не стало –
лучше даже не выглядывать в окно.
Не услышишь воробья или синицы –
уступили все пространство тракторам,
от грохочущих их гусениц не спится.
Лишь ворона хрипло каркнет по утрам.

3.
Здесь даже вороны – и те не живут,
лишь грохот и въедливый запах солярки,
растения сдали последний редут:
ни трав, ни деревьев, ни бабочки яркой.
Лишь серой земли развороченный пласт...
Неведомо, что здесь когда-нибудь будет,
но почва живого уже не создаст –
здесь мертвую зону устроили люди

The Dead Zone Arranged by People

1.
In even gray light without the slightest shining
Under the overcast sky,
All over the whole planet -
Tree trunks standing row by row
Fearing change and
as though probing sensitively
with their live antenna buds
our firmament which is just as fragile
as they are

Here there are Kapuletti and Montekki,
for them enmity is a habitual work:
woodcutters will come with their saws –
and the green ranks will fall.
And only then we will be horrified,
alas, by no means from shame,
on their graves we will suffocate,
we'll forever go after them.

2.
Perestroyka – how noisy was it earlier beyond the windows,
How the newspaper din began to accelerate
and the Troika bird flew into the unknown
to the shores coming through in the full dark

But soon it was gone out of our sight once again,
again the distant horizon became clouded,
the environment is almost gone -
better even not to look out the window.

You will not hear neither a sparrow nor a titbird -
they have given way to iron tractors all their space,
And one cannot sleep from their rattling caterpillars.
Only the crow croaks hoarsely at dawn.

3.
Here, even crows - and they do not live,
only the rumble and corrosive smell of diesel fuel,
plants surrendered the last redoubt:
no grass, no trees, no bright butterfly…
Only the turned reservoir of the gray carth ...
It is not known what there will ever be here,
But this soil will not ever create anything alive -
The dead zone was arranged by people.

Alla-Valeria Mikhalevich

Wandering the Anthropocene

for Max-Henry Moorhead

LED lights flickering
Microwaves emitting

Surveilling satellites vie for air ways
With cell phone frequencies

Rubble and soot-filled air
Like the 9/11 toxins everywhere

Devastated environments
Endless wars; careless industries

Once thriving communities dying
Bleached coral; flattened Mosul

Plastics and nuclear isotopes
Failed reactors; failed states

Failure to thrive
Shrinking ice; drought; floodwater coursing

Created scarcity
Our byproduct of greed

Seeds genetically modified
Mismanaged soil toxically fertilized

Humans displaced
Species disappeared

Searching for authenticity
With freedom from techno-tyranny

Striving for existence reclaimed
Community found in terms un-dictated

Kickstart organic motivation
Individuals must make the proclamation
to flourish

Marjorie Moorhead

An Earth Plea

you journey far and wide to glimpse the hidden parts of me
seeking out my waters, soils, wildlife and forests
captured in a snapshot
our harmonious existence
fixed
in glossy print

and yet
you don't really see me

the tumultuous, destructive, broken parts of me
the suffocation of my waters, soils, wildlife and forests
clasping poisoned ground
somehow we lost each other
strangers
in this changing climate

you are part water, mineral and dirt and therefore part world
I am the air that you breathe, the food that you eat
the water that runs through your veins
we are entangled and entwined
one
only you hold the power to save us

Vi Nguyen

Hurtling

after Hurricane Harvey Et al.

I

Don't bother; paper coffee
cups are plastic-lined

      & lidded; thin straws
for cold drinks ... Sea birds.
Turtles.

II

Waterfront Views FOR SALE:
Pay the Premium $$s
It's Prime!

(Where is. As is.)
You bet.

III

... Google Maps or *Leavin'*
on a Jet plane[1] — We send
regrets & news:

more CO_2. Live-streaming
      wildfires[2].

E.E. Nobbs

---

[1] John Denver's song
[2] Sep 06, 2017 – US EPA chief Scott Pruitt told CNN in an interview about Hurricane Irma **the time to talk about climate change** isn't now.

Planet Earth II

after David Attenborough

Planet Earth II is thinner than ever
Planet Earth II contains the following upgrades and bug fixes:
     Interfaith dialogue
     Patience
     Context
     Colour-blind police
     Infinite non-renewable energy sources
     Only your favourite foods
     Only your favourite people
     Only tolerable music
     2016 removed as causing problems for some users
     Enhanced type face
     Compliments-only setting
     As many chances as you need
     As many bullets as you need

Planet Earth II has had the headphone jack removed
Planet Earth II is now remorse-free
Planet Earth II also comes with:
     Sleep mode
     Benefit of the doubt
     Unlimited hindsight
     Free wi-fi
     The ability to add or remove children
     Loneliness-to-wisdom converter
     Compulsory sport
     Compulsory art
     Compulsory empathy
     No first-hand shops
     1 complimentary hug at the beginning and end of each
     day
     Peanut Butter now tax-deductible

All toilets unisex
All colours gender neutral

Planet Earth II was designed in California and assembled in
China
Planet Earth II is repayable in easy monthly instalments
Planet Earth II allows you to love the right person first time
round
Planet Earth II contains no small print
Planet Earth II is all small print
Planet Earth II is only sunrises
Planet Earth II is only destinations
Planet Earth II is only Ts and Cs
Planet Earth II reserves the right to
Planet Earth II begs the question
Planet Earth II is yours for just
Planet Earth II is currently out-of-stock

Ben Norris

Zest

Take one from the bowl.
Hold it in your palm, navel up, as if
still growing; as though it were the world.
Let in the nail of your thumb.
Take care; the rind must come off in one.
Even blind, you can circumnavigate
its umbilicus, peel away ice fields,
tundra, blue-eyed iris grass and krill.

The orange flesh will turn, its pith
orbiting as fingers strip forests
holding undiscovered rain,
Appalachian fens, snowshoe hares.
There goes a shining sunrise
ocean, great clouds of silver fish.
Birds screech as they wheel
around a spiralling of rind.

Don't stop; there's more to pare.
Red deer; blue oyster mushrooms
letting go their spores.
Now open out the fleshy sphere,
its unexploded sacs of seed.
The empty rind will wind back up,
appear intact. To implode will take
some time. By then you will be gone.

Michael Ray

Crab

On Henderson Island[1]
pictures show a hermit crab in a plastic cup
its plated body wedged into the hard sides,
the red of a ketchup bottle.
Perhaps it is suitable, this vessel -
it is light, clean, smooth -
the crab drags its plastic home along the sand
its claws are black and armoured
they extend sensitively, retract,
the light inside the plastic is dilute,
red, smells of hot polymer and salt -
the crab and its home make an interesting track on the sand -
pristine sand, or so it appears -
on closer inspection it seems the cup is stackable,
part of a child's toy,
a tower of many colours, each cup to be placed
upon another, so it locks together
to be knocked down and built and knocked down again
until we all turn away, bored.

Sarah Westcott

---

[1] Henderson Island, in the South Pacific, is one of the most remote places in the world, and also one of the most polluted.

Geography Lessons

I.

At school I teach the girls
the four main forms of river erosion.

I give them a diagram with features:
meander, silt-bed, banks with cracks, mud creases —

they agree it's likely the four forms in combination
that give the river its bent, its curl.

What about flood plains, I ask, what about oxbow islands?
What about the undoing of land in the night

and the swallowing of whole houses into mud?
Huge as these losses are I want them to understand

the greatest losses start in smaller.

II.

After five days of rain
a boy dies mining coltan.

In our module on Fair Trade
we talk about cocoa pods.

Here's a photo of a cocoa pod,
here's another of several pods drying

and a farmer's hand shucking segments
like a kid cracks slices of Toblerone on Christmas.

I give out census results, GDP and grid paper,
if the red line goes up, I tell them, we call that progress.

Tomorrow we'll map precipitation
at given points across the equator.

They know how to plot five days of rain
in bar graphs and line charts

but what units should I give them
to explain the wrong kind of downpour

at the wrong time of year?
The mud that it makes,

the way it swallows the rungs.

III.

I used to believe in knowledge
as something to aim for –

a field beyond the woods
where a hedge and the wheat

touched hands, made cornflowers.

I didn't know knowledge is more like a vase,
how its internal structures of doubt

can be worked to the point of collapse.

What do we do now with all these broken pieces,
the body of air that leaks out?

Mariah Whelan

Eschaton

The last Christian clings to his floating plank
under the oriflammes of a warmed-up world… Long since
all towns became Venice or
shut their doors, desiccated… And choked on dust.
        The oscillations
and mass migrations… But he remembers ice.

Now a turquoise continent of sea… All being
and all change… What profits him? And how shall the fallen
rise? When Christ, having discarded
his own plank, leaves a shining footprint on
        the shining wave
with no-one left to save except the jellyfish floating

over the fields and cities… A great pierced hand to cup
the waters… And the risen waters stretch wide their jaws.
Hell is a muddy, wet place; a broken
second covenant never to kill by drowning…
        mayhap under
the sundering caffè latte sky… Burning… Waves brown

with laved away topsoil… And in the hollow bowel
of the brown dead world-sea lies the incorruptible corpse
of brother-lover Lazarus in the world-
sea-tomb, human Lazarus, the priceless pearl
        sleeping cloistered
in its oyster, whose sores are ores of gold…

And the Son-Sun deigning to tread the murky
waters of a murdered Earth as once he walked Galilee.
Deer lick a saint's tomb daily at noon.
Price tags on ex-possessions of the dead.
 Silenced cathedral
and polyhedral macrocosm... And so to bed.

Andrew Paul Wood

Contributors

Suzi Attree has a PhD in medieval literature and a passion for the natural world and the role people play within it. She works as Development Manager at Oxford Brookes University, which allows her to be immersed in science, the arts and ecology, and learn astounding facts about the world every day.

S.B. Banks' work has appeared in *Louisiana Literature*, *The Tulane Review*, and *The Madison Review*. He volunteers with Citizens' Climate Lobby, and he remains optimistic.

Camille Brantes was born in 1986 in Avignon (France). At 21, he moved to Taiwan where he studied classical Chinese literature. He lives and works in Paris today and participates in many public poetry readings as a poet or translator.

Michael Conley is a poet and teacher based in Manchester. His first poetry pamphlet, *Aquarium*, was published by Flarestack and his second, *More Weight*, is with Eyewear.

Emily Cotterill grew up in Alfreton, Derbyshire and moved to Cardiff to be close to a different coalfield and the Manic Street Preachers. Her poetry has appeared in various locations in print and online, including on display in Winchester Cathedral and during Literacy Hour in a Derbyshire primary school.

Julian Dobson lives in Sheffield. His poems have appeared in publications including *Magma*, *Brittle Star* and *Acumen*, and on a bus in Guernsey.

Carrie Etter is a Reader in Creative Writing at Bath Spa University. Her third collection, *Imagined Sons* (Seren, 2014), was shortlisted for the Ted Hughes Award for New Work in Poetry, and her fourth collection, *The Weather in Normal* (Seren, 2018), will include the poem featured in this collection.

Nathan Evans is a writer, director and performer whose work in film and theatre has been funded by the Arts Council, toured by the British Council, broadcast on Channel 4, archived in the BFI Mediatheque and picked up some statuettes. His first poetry collection, *Threads*, is published by Inkandescent.

Matt Girling is an Artist, activist, comic creator and a Children's television prop maker, living and working in Manchester. His practice involves film making, sculpture, animation, performance, music and interactive happenings but his mane preoccupation has always been drawing and illustrating. You can find him online at: www.mattgirlingartist.tumblr.com

Kim Goldberg is the author of seven books of poetry and nonfiction. She holds a degree in biology, is an avid birdwatcher, and organized an eco-poetry panel and workshop for the inaugural Cascadia Poetry Festival in Seattle. She lives on Vancouver Island and online at www.pigsquash.wordpress.com.

Amlanjyoti Goswami's poems have appeared in publications in India, Nepal, the UK, Hong Kong, South Africa, Kenya and the USA, including *Forty under Forty: An Anthology of Post-Globalisation Poetry* (Poetrywala, 2016). He grew up in Guwahati, Assam and now lives in Delhi.

Sam Illingworth is a Senior Lecturer in Science Communication at Manchester Metropolitan University, where his research involves developing dialogue between scientists and non-scientists. He mainly does this through the use of poetry and games. As a spoken word artist, he has performed all over the world, including the Edinburgh Fringe, the Green Man music festival, and with the Royal Shakespeare Company. You can find out more about his research, and read some of his poems by visiting his website: www.samillingworth.com

Catriona Knapman is a Scottish writer and human rights worker who has lived in four continents. She has published widely in the UK and abroad and brought her first show 'Out On The World' to the Edinburgh Fringe 2016, where she won second place in the StAnza Best Poem of the Fringe Award.

Valérie Masson-Delmotte is a climate scientist based in Paris Saclay, France, and currently co-chair of the Intergovernmental Panel on Climate Change for the working group on the physical science basis of climate change. Her own research activity is linked to climate imprints in natural archives such as ice cores. She is learning from past climate response to perturbations and past climate variability to understand how the climate system operates, to test our ability to model these responses, and therefore to inform on confidence in projections of future climate change. She has also written books for children and for the general public, as part of her diverse outreach activities. Her research and engagement for outreach have been acknowledged by several prizes in France and abroad.

Alla-Valeria Mikhalevich is a Professor in Biology, corresponding Member of European Academy of Sciences, Arts and Literature, of International Pen-Club, member of EUROSCIENCE, the Grzybowski Foundation, SPASS, the Union of Writers of Petersburg and Russia. She is known in literature as a poet and translator from English, translating Sheamus Heaney, as well as other Irish and American poets.

Marjorie Moorhead's poem grew from conversation with her son, as well as thinking of Stevie Wonder's song, 'Pastime Paradise'. Marjorie has work forthcoming in poetry collections from The Blueline Press, and Hobblebush Press. She lives near woods, mountains and rivers in NH, USA.

Helen Mort was born in Sheffield. Her first collection *Division Street* won the Fenton Aldeburgh Prize. Her second collection *No Map Could Show Them* (Chatto & Windus) is a PBS Recommendation. She blogs at *Freefall*, her first novel is forthcoming from Chatto in 2019, and she lectures in Creative Writing at Manchester Metropolitan University.

Vi Nguyen works in science communication to bridge the gap between research and the public. She is passionate about the use of effective communications to raise awareness of important global issues and to create dialogue to facilitate positive change.

E.E. Nobbs lives in Charlottetown, Prince Edward Island, Canada. She's had a book of poetry published - *The Invisible Girl,* grew up on a farm and has worked many years as an entomology research technician. Find out more at her website & blog: www.ellyfromearth.wordpress.com/.

Ben Norris is a writer, actor, and two-time national poetry slam champion, whose verse has taken him everywhere from Latitude to the Royal Albert Hall. His debut solo show, 'The Hitchhiker's Guide to the Family', won the IdeasTap Underbelly Award and his first short film, for Channel 4, saw him nominated for Best New Talent at the Royal Television Society Awards.

Michael Ray is a poet and glass artist living in Southern Ireland. His poems have appeared in a number of Irish and international journals.

Dan Simpson is a poet, performer, and producer making highly engaging and contemporary work on subjects including science and technology; history and place; geek culture and videogames; people and poetry. Dan has appeared at popular science events and talks, as well as Glastonbury, Roundhouse, and on the BBC. A former Canterbury Laureate, his first collection is *Applied Mathematics* from Burning Eye Books. He can be found online at www.dansimpsonpoet.co.uk.

Sarah Westcott's first collection *Slant Light* was published by Pavilion Poetry in 2016 and a poem from the book was Highly Commended in the Forward Prizes. She was a poet-in-residence at the Bethnal Green Nature Reserve in London, and Manchester Cathedral poet of the year in 2016.

Mariah Whelan is a poet based in the Centre for New Writing at The University of Manchester where she writes poems and researches traumatic memory in Irish fiction.

Andrew Paul Wood is a cultural critic, art historian and writer based in Christchurch, New Zealand.

23169006R00029

Printed in Poland
by Amazon Fulfillment
Poland Sp. z o.o., Wrocław